Gunn

by Harry Conroy

LangSyne
PUBLISHING
WRITING *to* REMEMBER

Lang**Syne**

PUBLISHING

WRITING *to* REMEMBER

79 Main Street, Newtongrange,
Midlothian EH22 4NA
Tel: 0131 344 0414   Fax: 0845 075 6085
E-mail: info@lang-syne.co.uk
www.langsyneshop.co.uk

Design by Dorothy Meikle
Printed by Printwell Ltd
© Lang Syne Publishers Ltd 2017

All rights reserved. No part of this publication may be reproduced, stored
or introduced into a retrieval system, or transmitted in any form or by any
means (electronic, mechanical, photocopying, recording or otherwise) without
the prior written permission of Lang Syne Publishers Ltd.

ISBN 978-1-85217-094-3

Gunn

SEPT NAMES INCLUDE:

Enrick
Gallie
Jamieson
Kean
MacCorkill
MacKean
MacManus
MacWilliam
Mann
Manson
Nelson
Robinson
Ronaldson
Swan
Williamson
Wilson
Wylie

Gunn

MOTTO:
Aut pax aut bellum
(Either Peace or War).

CREST:
A dexter hand wielding a sword
in bend proper.

TERRITORY:
Caithness and Sutherland.

Chapter one:

The origins of the clan system

by Rennie McOwan

The original Scottish clans of the Highlands and the great families of the Lowlands and Borders were gatherings of families, relatives, allies and neighbours for mutual protection against rivals or invaders.

Scotland experienced invasion from the Vikings, the Romans and English armies from the south. The Norman invasion of what is now England also had an influence on land-holding in Scotland. Some of these invaders stayed on and in time became 'Scottish'.

The word clan derives from the Gaelic language term 'clann', meaning children, and it was first used many centuries ago as communities were formed around tribal lands in glens and mountain fastnesses.

The format of clans changed over the centuries, but at its best the chief and his family held the land on behalf of all, like trustees, and the ordinary clansmen and women believed they had a blood relationship with the founder of their clan.

There were two way duties and obligations. An inadequate chief could be deposed and replaced by someone of greater ability.

Clan people had an immense pride in race. Their relationship with the chief was like adult children to a father and they had a real dignity.

The concept of clanship is very old and a more feudal notion of authority gradually crept in.

Pictland, for instance, was divided into seven principalities ruled by feudal leaders who were the strongest and most charismatic leaders of their particular groups.

By the sixth century the 'British' kingdoms of Strathclyde, Lothian and Celtic Dalriada (Argyll) had emerged and Scotland, as one nation, began to take shape in the time of King Kenneth MacAlpin.

Some chiefs claimed descent from

ancient kings which may not have been accurate
in every case.

By the twelfth and thirteenth centuries the
clans and families were more strongly brought
under the central control of Scottish monarchs.

Lands were awarded and administered
more and more under royal favour, yet the power
of the area clan chiefs was still very great.

The long wars to ensure Scotland's
independence against the expansionist ideas of
English monarchs extended the influence of some
clans and reduced the lands of others.

Those who supported Scotland's greatest
king, Robert the Bruce, were awarded the
territories of the families who had opposed his
claim to the Scottish throne.

In the Scottish Borders country – the
notorious Debatable Lands – the great families
built up a ferocious reputation for providing
warlike men accustomed to raiding into England
and occasionally fighting one another.

Chiefs had the power to dispense justice
and to confiscate lands and clan warfare produced

a society where martial virtues – courage, hardiness, tenacity – were greatly admired.

Gradually the relationship between the clans and the Crown became strained as Scottish monarchs became more orientated to life in the Lowlands and, on occasion, towards England.

The Highland clans spoke a different language, Gaelic, whereas the language of Lowland Scotland and the court was Scots and in more modern times, English.

Highlanders dressed differently, had different customs, and their wild mountain land sometimes seemed almost foreign to people living in the Lowlands.

It must be emphasised that Gaelic culture was very rich and story-telling, poetry, piping, the clarsach (harp) and other music all flourished and were greatly respected.

Highland culture was different from other parts of Scotland but it was not inferior or less sophisticated.

Central Government, whether in London or Edinburgh, sometimes saw the Gaelic clans as

"The spirit of the clan means much to thousands of people"

a challenge to their authority and some sent expeditions into the Highlands and west to crush the power of the Lords of the Isles.

Nevertheless, when the eighteenth century Jacobite Risings came along the cause of the Stuarts was mainly supported by Highland clans.

The word Jacobite comes from the Latin for James – Jacobus. The Jacobites wanted to restore the exiled Stuarts to the throne of Britain.

The monarchies of Scotland and England became one in 1603 when King James VI of Scotland (1st of England) gained the English throne after Queen Elizabeth died.

The Union of Parliaments of Scotland and England, the Treaty of Union, took place in 1707.

Some Highland clans, of course, and Lowland families opposed the Jacobites and supported the incoming Hanoverians.

After the Jacobite cause finally went down at Culloden in 1746 a kind of ethnic cleansing took place. The power of the chiefs was curtailed. Tartan and the pipes were banned in law.

Many emigrated, some because they

wanted to, some because they were evicted by force. In addition, many Highlanders left for the cities of the south to seek work.

Many of the clan lands became home to sheep and deer shooting estates.

But the warlike traditions of the clans and the great Lowland and Border families lived on, with their descendants fighting bravely for freedom in two world wars.

Remember the men from whence you came, says the Gaelic proverb, and to that could be added the role of many heroic women.

The spirit of the clan, of having roots, whether Highland or Lowland, means much to thousands of people.

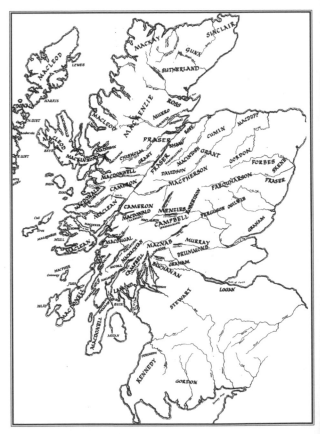

A map of the clans' homelands

Chapter two:

Viking warriors

The Clan Gunn originated around the end of the twelfth century. They claim to be descended from Olaf the Black, Norse King of Man and the Isles who died in 1237.

Olaf's second son Gunni came to Scotland towards the end of the twelfth century. The name Gunni meant 'war' which befitted the Norse prince who is described in the annals of history as a great Viking warrior. He married Ragnhild, sister of Harald, Jarl of Orkney, whose wife was descended from St. Ragnvald, founder of the great cathedral of St. Magnus at Kirkwall. Ragnhild inherited estates in Caithness from her brother and it was there she and Gunni settled.

The clan territory, with its roots in Caithness, lay on the border between the lands of the Earls of Sutherland and the Earls of Caithness, while to the west lay Strathnaver, the territory of the Mackays or Lord Reays country.

The Gunns extended their territory at the expense of their neighbours until the fifteenth century when the tables were turned on them and they were driven from their territories by the surrounding clans. The Gunns fled from Caithness and settled on the lands of Kildonan in Sutherland.

George Gunn Crouner, or Coroner, of Caithness in the fifteenth century is the first person to appear in records credited with the title Clan Chief. The proper Celtic patronymic of the Gunn Chiefs was Mac Sheumais Chataich, but George Gunn was better known as Am Braisdeach Mor, The Great Brooch Wearer, so called after the insignia he wore as coroner. He lived in great splendour in his castle at Clyth and held court there in a manner that rivalled any of the Highland Chiefs.

Chapter three:

Bitter enemies

The Gunns were the sworn enemies of the Keiths, who challenged them both in the influence they wielded and the land they ruled. The Keiths held sway from their stronghold, Akergill Castle.

The constant feuding between the two clans was bloody, with both sides suffering heavy losses. Power and wealth were the underlying motivation for the bloodshed but both claimed moral justification for their deeds.

The fate of Helen, daughter of Gunn of Braemor who was much admired by Dugald Keith is a prime example of this behaviour. Helen Gunn completely rebuffed all Dugald's overtures and instead agreed to be married to another man. On hearing this a jealous Dugald promptly laid siege to her family home, killing many of the inhabitants, and abducted the poor girl, imprisoning her in Ackergill Castle. The episode ended in tragedy when Helen Gunn in desperation threw herself from the tower rather than submit to Dugald Keith's demands.

The Gunns continued to raid Keith territory but they suffered defeats in 1438 at the battle of Tannach Moor and again in 1464 at Dirlot in Strathmore. However both clans sustained considerable losses and eventually agreed to settle their differences by having a battle of champions.

A remote spot in Strathmore was chosen for the fight to the death. It was agreed that only 12 horse should represent each Clan

The Gunns arrived at the agreed spot to be confronted by double their number. The wily Keiths had mounted two men to each horse thus outnumbering their opponents two to one. This trickery enraged the Gunns who despite their disadvantage hurled themselves at the Keiths in a fury, giving good account of themselves. Both sides fought till they could fight no longer. At the end of the battle Coroner George and four of his sons lay dead.

James, the Coroner's only surviving son, succeeded his father as Chief, but had to flee Caithness with his clan to Sutherland, where their chief dwelling was Killernan in the parish of Kildonan.

It is from James the patronymic of Mac-Sheumais or MacKeamish (that is, the son of James) was derived which then became the Gaelic sept name of the chief.

Almost one hundred years later James's son, William, avenged his grandfather's death by killing Keith of Akergill, his son and twelve followers at Drummoy in Sutherland.

Chapter four:

Ambush at Ben Grian

**The Gunns' neighbours were again tiring of
the constant warring with the clan and
the Earls of Caithness and Sutherland,
both having lost their patience with the
marauding clan, entered into a pact to
destroy the Gunns.**

The plot was probably sealed at
Grinigoe Castle around 1586 when it was
agreed to attack the clan simultaneously from
either side and to encircle them to prevent
escape. The plan went astray when the
Sinclairs of Caithness came upon the Gunns on
the slopes of Ben Grian and observing that
their enemy were relatively few in number
decided to attack without waiting for the
Sutherlands as planned.

The crafty Gunns however had chosen
their position wisely. They waited until the
Sinclairs had exhausted themselves on the

steep ascent then rained arrows into them at close quarters, killing the commander and 120 of his men. Routed, the Sinclairs turned and fled down the slopes of the mountain, pursued by the Gunns till night fell.

The Earl of Sutherland repaired this defeat by following the Gunns to the shores of Loch Broom where it was the turn of the Gunns to be defeated with 32 clansmen falling on the battlefield and their captain, George Gunn, taken prisoner.

Despite their best efforts the two Earls failed to wipe out the Gunns. The beleaguered clan strengthened their bonds with the MacKays when Gunn of Killearnan married Mary , sister of Lord Reay, the Mackay chief, and the following Gunn chief married Lord Reay's daughter. It was the son of this marriage, commonly known as Donald Crottach, the hunchback, who became the 6th chief of the Gunns. It was during his period of chieftainship that the clan seat at Killearnan was burnt to the ground, apparently by accident, and debt

finally did what their enemies could not do –
stripped the clan of their lands around
Killearnan.

From the original Caithness Gunns
many Septs of the clan were established.

From James's son William are descended
the Wilsons of Caithness, from Robert who
was killed with his father the Gun Robsons and
from John also killed, the Gun MacLeans, or
Macians, that is Johnsons of Caithness.

Chapter five:

Highland Clearances

About the time the lands of Killearnan were lost another branch of the clan were on the ascent. William, brother of the chief of Robert's descendants the Gunns of Brae-more, known as the Robson Gunns, fought in the army of the King of Sweden.

He rose to command a battalion. Later, while fighting for Charles I in 1639, he was knighted. He returned to the Continent to serve the Holy Roman Empire and marry a German Baroness. He became an Imperial General and was created a baron of the Holy Roman Empire in 1649. Eventually debt was also to claim the lands of Braemore but not until the end of the eighteenth century.

When the rallying call went out during the 1745 Jacobite uprising for the Highland clans to support the Stuart bid for the throne by pledging their allegiance to Bonnie Prince Charlie the Gunns did not fight for the Prince. Instead they joined the

The Highland Clearances

Hanoverians. The eighth clan chief reinforced the clan's links with the House of Hanover by serving as a regular Highland officer in the British army. He was eventually killed fighting in India.

Ironically, considering their many generations of feuding and their warlike nature, the death knell of the clan was brought about by the docile sheep and the onset of the Highland Clearances.

Between 1811 and 1831 sheep were introduced onto the land. The traditional clan system began to break down when clan chiefs laid personal claim to the clan lands, which had always been considered to be owned by the entire community. The chiefs became true lairds and forced people to leave their homes to make way for sheep.

Families were made homeless as the Laird's agents torched their homes.

The people were then forced to the coast where ships were anchored offshore to transport them to the four corners of the earth. They were herded like cattle onto the ships and many died before reaching their destinations in North America and Australia.

Those who were not transported overseas fled south to the lowlands of Scotland or into the heart of England. The exiled clansmen were never to again see the homeland that so many of them had fought so long and hard to keep.

Scotland's loss, however, was the rest of the world's gain. The name of Gunn was to become common in several parts of the world. Gunns who could trace their ancestry back to the remote glens of Sutherland rose to prominence in their new communities.

Meanwhile, Gunns of note through the centuries include: Barnabas Gunn, musical composer, who was organist of Chelsea Hospital when he died in 1753; John Gunn, author of several musical works, found fame in the eighteenth century; William Gunn, an Episcopalian clergyman, became an antiquarian writer of note in the early nineteenth century; Daniel Gunn, a congregational minister was celebrated for his unemotional style of preaching and his schools at Christchurch in Hampshire; and Robert Gunn, the naturalist, became Superintendent of prisons in Tasmania.

Chapter six:

Secrets of Castle Gunn

The earliest known castle of the Clan Gunn stood on a rock facing the cliffs at Clyth, seven miles south of Wick. It is thought to have been established in the mid-thirteenth century by Snaekoll Gunni.

The foundations of the keep are now barely discernible standing on the cliff edge on what is a forbidding site. Winter gales, storms and difficult tides would have made access by boat difficult at various times of the year, and there is speculation that there was also a draw-bridge to the mainland. There is still evidence of a rough stair cut into the rock on the mainland cliffs which would have allowed access to the castle from the foreshore, but this approach would not have been used to supply the strong-hold with fuel, weapons, food etc.

A painting by Andrew Spratt shows the keep rising to three storeys in height with a timber palisade. The foundations give an indication of the strength of the defenses, measuring 37 x 23ft externally, with walls some 3ft thick.

Castle Gunn's existence was short-lived after one of the Gunns, thought to be James de Gun's father Ottar, married the daughter of the King of Norway, despite being already married. He arranged the sinking of the ship carrying the Norwegian Princess to Scotland with her dowry. Legend has it that a pot of gold was washed up on a nearby rock which lead to it being named 'leac an oir' – flagstone of the gold.

The Norwegian King took his revenge, slaying Ottar and setting fire to the castle. The castle was rebuilt but by the end of the thirteenth century it was found to be too small and abandoned in favour of Castle Halberry, a mile to the South. The stone from the abandoned castle was used to build a causeway at a nearby harbour.

Conclusion:

The present day

The clan's eighth chief was killed in action in India while serving as an officer in the British army, leaving the chieftainship to pass to a cousin whose descendants carried on the line until the nineteenth century when the 10th MacSheumais Chataich died without leaving an heir.

Although scattered throughout the world the clan is at present led by a Commander, Iain Gunn, who has been appointed by the Lord Lyon King of Arms.

Iain is a descendant of a seventeenth century laird. Recently petitions have been presented to the Lord Lyon with a view to seeking representation to the bloodline chiefs and it is hoped that a successful claimant will be found. Perhaps the valiant Gunns will be able to establish their Highland roots yet again.

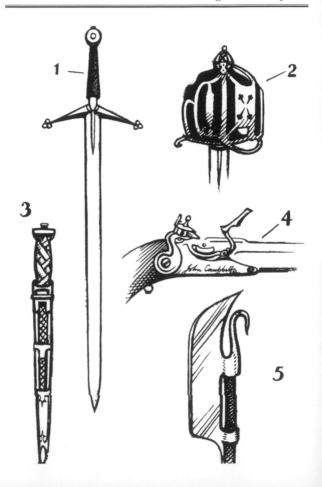

Highland weapons

1) The claymore or two-handed sword
   (fifteenth or early sixteenth century)

2) Basket hilt of broadsword
   made in Stirling, 1716

3) Highland dirk
   (eighteenth century)

4) Steel pistol *(detail)* made in Doune

5) Head of Lochaber Axe as carried
   in the '45 and earlier

GATHERING OF THE CLANS

CLAN MEMORABILIA FROM LANG SYNE

Books, postcards, Teddy bears, keyrings, mugs and much more...

Visit our website:
www.langsyneshop.co.uk

or write to us:
**Lang Syne Publishing,
79 Main Street, Newtongrange,
Midlothian EH22 4NA
Tel: 0131 344 0414   Fax: 0845 075 6085
E-mail: info@lang-syne.co.uk**